T0197060

Gossip

Gossip
"The Intent to Kill"

Jacqueline Stewart

authorHOUSE®

AuthorHouse™
1663 Liberty Drive
Bloomington, IN 47403
www.authorhouse.com
Phone: 1-800-839-8640

Published by AuthorHouse   06/25/2012

ISBN: 978-1-4772-3172-2 (sc)
ISBN: 978-1-4772-3171-5 (e)

Library of Congress Control Number: 2012911502

Any people depicted in stock imagery provided by Thinkstock are models, and such images are being used for illustrative purposes only.
Certain stock imagery © Thinkstock.

This book is printed on acid-free paper.

Because of the dynamic nature of the Internet, any web addresses or links contained in this book may have changed since publication and may no longer be valid. The views expressed in this work are solely those of the author and do not necessarily reflect the views of the publisher, and the publisher hereby disclaims any responsibility for them.

This book is dedicated to my parents, Word of Truth church and Patrice Morrison. You all have given me the tools to walk in to my destiny.

Acknowledgements

I would like to thank my husband, Antoine Stewart for unknowingly placing me on my road to destiny. To my daughter Ahriel, the birth of your life has pushed me in to a deeper spiritual level in God. I love you. I would also like to thank my parents, Ernest and Deloris White; you have never ceased in believing in me, and have always made me feel like I could be and do anything. Frank and Nelda Ebarb thank you for your support throughout the years. Being connected to your ministry has taken me places, as a young kid, I never thought I would go. Pastor and Co-pastor Ail and Lisa Harris thank you for encouraging me to write my first play. That idea catapulted me into greater territory. I want the world to know how much I value family so to all of my sisters, brothers, nieces, nephews, uncles, aunts, cousins, grandparents and friends, I love you. To one cousin Patrice, thank you for speaking life in to me when I felt nearly spiritually and emotionally dead. God used you as a mid-wife to birth this book out of me.

Contents

Chapter Ten

Part 3: How to RecoverFrom Gossip

Introduction

"Introducing Gossip"

I would like to dedicate this book to my intended weapon of demise "Gossip," and if you're reading this book your intended weapon of demise as well. God has fashioned, designed and prepared you for such a time as this. This is your season to grow, and thank God for your enemies because they are helping you to do it.

The Word of God in *Jeremiah 29: 11 says, "For I know the thoughts that I think toward you, saith the Lord, thoughts of peace, and not evil, to give you an expected end (KJV)."*

Do you know the thoughts that the Lord has toward you? Are you in full understanding of those thoughts, and of God's purpose for your life? The enemy definitely is aware of God's purpose for you, and that is why he is seeking to destroy you. The enemy knows that you have authority, power, the anointing of God and the Word of God living and active on the inside of you, he is trying any and every way to kill your spirit. Don't be surprised when the attempt act of murder comes by way of friends, family members, church folks, co-workers etc. Whomever he can use he will, but thank God that God's people are more the conquerors through Christ, Jesus. We are the head and not the tail, and above only and not beneath. Don't let the Devil kill you!

John 4:4 says, "But you belong to God, my dear children. You have already won a victory over those people, because the spirit who lives in you is greater than the spirit who lives in the world" (NLT).

In this book, I will discuss how Gossip or the spirit of Gossip is an attempt to annihilate the purpose of God in you. Facing this demon has given me insight, knowledge, wisdom and even more so **POWER**. When we as God's people become aware of those things that are trying to oppress us, we gain **POWER**. You may ask "why does she say we will gain power?" You will gain power because once you know and understand the avenue of attack by the enemy, and seek God on wisdom on how to defeat it, and then actually defeat it; you won't be able to be ambushed by that way of avenue again. Now, you have gained wisdom and spiritual insight, therefore the enemy can't defeat or trap you. Your gained knowledge and wisdom has given you **POWER**.

Here is a definition that I have come up with concerning Gossip: **Gossip causes feelings of distress, embarrassment, shame, fear, restraint, one's unwillingness to move forward, confusion, discomfort, complication, difficulty and no support. Gossip can drive a person into a place of desolation, isolation, depression, lack of trust, lack of companionship and remoteness of human habitation (from being around others).**

Look at the damage that gossip causes! It is literally trying to cause damage to the point of no return to the person or persons that it has set out against . . . it's intent is to kill. In this book I will discuss the effects of Gossip, the places where it can cause you to run and how to overcome the spirit. I pray that as you read this book that you will be restored and repaired. I thank God that your deliverance has come.

Part 1

The Harmful Effects of Gossip

Chapter One

"I am sending you out like sheep among wolves. Therefore be as shrewd as snakes and as innocent as doves"—Matthew 10:16 (NIV).

If you are anything how I use to be, gullible and naïve it's time for you to wise up! Let's dissect the scripture above. The first sentence of the Word of the Lord says, *"I am sending you out like sheep among the wolves."* God has and is sending His people out to places where there are others that may not think like we do. He has sent you out child of God among people that don't think like you. when I say "that don't think like you," I mean that God has sent you out among people that don't possess the heart of God, the spirit of God, the character of God and/or the truth of God. How will you know if they don't possess the heart of God? The Word says that you will know them by their fruit. You will know them by what they do or do not produce.

As we continue to read, the second sentence tells us *"therefore be as shrewd as snakes and as innocent as doves."* Since we have been sent out in to a dishonest world, we must be wise as serpents. Most people when they think about the character of a snake, they think of it as being conniving and that is partly true, but we are not to take on the character of being conniving. We are to take on the character of a snake that is wise, insightful and discerning.

The word of God says, *"And God saw everything that he had made, and, behold, it was very good"—Genesis 1:31 (KJV).*

Upon creating the serpent, even God saw that it was good. He created the serpent to be a wise creature, but of course when the enemy came he came to distort that which was good in to something bad. God tells us to learn from the wisdom of the serpent and not from its deception.

Finally, the end of the verse says we are to be *"innocent as doves."* In our possessing wisdom, we must also possess meekness and humility. Have you ever heard a person use the phrase "don't take my kindness for a weakness?" The world and people that don't possess the spirit of God may think that being kind and loving, or even quiet is being weak but don't be fooled. Tell your enemies that your kindness, love and silence is you walking in wisdom."

Why must we take heed to this scripture and pray to God for wisdom, insight and discernment? I had to learn that even though I may possess the spirit and heart of God, others may not; and even though I may be faithful, loyal and honest or have good character others may not. What am I saying? Basically, as a wise old person would say, "you can't trust any and everybody." You have to discern the heart of those that are trying to come in connection with you, and those that you have already made the connection. If need be, you have to annihilate the conniving snakes in your life. God will show you who is against you, but it is up to you to listen and to separate yourself.

Have you ever confided in a person, and you thought the conversation was just between the two of you? Or maybe you had an issue with someone, you talked to the person about it and you thought the situation had been settled. Lord knows I have! All of a sudden you start to notice that people who once liked you or that was friendly towards you started to treat you differently. You're thinking to yourself what is wrong . . . did I do or say something? The truth is you didn't, but Gossip did. Instead of leaving the conversation between you and them, they went and Gossiped about you. Not only did they Gossip about what was said, they added on to it, manipulated it and even made up stories about you. They went as far as to completely lie about your very person. Their intentions saints of God were to embarrass you and to send you running. Listen to me, don't run and don't move out of place! Your enemies want your stuff, and once you move they will move in. Let's listen to what the Word of the Lord says about Gossip.

"Do not spread false reports. Do not help a wicked man by being a malicious witness"—exodus 23:1 (NIV).

The Word calls Gossip a malicious witness. What does malicious mean? Malicious means having or showing a desire to cause harm to someone. Gossip is a malicious witnesses desiring to cause great harm to your life and to the plans that God has set for you; tell it to "watch out" because it is not you who it's coming against, but the hand of God. With that being said, pray for Gossip's deliverance because who would want to come against God almighty.

Proverbs 25:18 says, "Telling lies about others is as harmful as hitting them with an ax, wounding them with a sword, or shooting them with a sharp arrow" (NLT).

In this text, Gossip is being compared to as being like hitting someone with an ax, wounding them with a sword or shooting them with an arrow. OUCH, how painful! I would think that if a person tried to cut me with an ax or sword, or shoot me with an arrow that they would be trying to kill me, and I'm pretty sure you're thinking the same thing. Gossip causes disfiguration, it messes up who you really are on the inside. Because of Gossip, people now only see what they think is a mess of who you are, instead of how the Father has created you. I want to reiterate what I said in the introduction about Gossip, so we can flow into the upcoming chapters of the book.

Gossip causes feelings of distress, embarrassment, shame, fear, restraint, one's unwillingness to move forward, confusion, discomfort, complication, difficulty and no support. Gossip can drive a person into a place of desolation, isolation, depression, lack of trust, lack of companionship and remoteness of human habitation (from being around others).

Children of the Lord continue to read through each chapter, because now you're headed down the road of recovery from Gossip's intended demise for your life.

Chapter Two

Embarrassment and Shame, Fear and Distress

Gossip's intent is to make you feel as if though you have done or said something wrong. If you allow Gossip to make you feel that way when you know honestly in your heart you haven't done or said anything wrong, it will have power over you to make you and keep you silent. Gossip will try to keep you from being who you really are. It will try to have you bound in deep fear and worry to the point of feeling like anything you do or say will be taken wrongly; or will be talked about . . . Gossiped about. People of God there is nothing shameful about you, and God didn't create you to hide. I love the song where it says, "I'm trading my shame for the joy of the Lord!" Look at what Paul writes.

"We are pressed on every side by troubles, but we are not crushed. We are perplexed, but not driven to despair"—2 Corinthians 4:8 (NLT).

The enemy is trying to press you in every way that he can. He is trying to press you with embarrassment and shame so hard to the point where you become mute. Satan is trying to have you perplexed and confused, and wondering "God what is happening to me? What are you doing? Where are you Lord?" But the Word of the Lord says that you are not crushed nor driven to despair.

Let's take a moment to pray:

Lord, I come to you standing on your Word. The enemy is trying to confuse me and is trying to cause me to run. Lord, you are the solid rock and on you, I will stand. Father, you said in Isaiah 26:3, "You keep him in perfect peace whose mind is stayed on you, because he trusts you" (ESV). God I place my heart and mind on you. I trust you, and know that this is my season to grow. Like Paul said, I'm pressed but not crushed; I'm perplexed but not driven to despair. In Jesus' name I pray. Amen.

There is nothing like a prayer to keep you moving forward. Remember that prayer is your charger. Jesus would go in to the wilderness away from the multitudes to pray. He knew that He needed to be charged. As He prayed to the Father, He was endowed with power. You now have been endowed with strength and power to keep moving to what's ahead.

Have you ever been so fearful to the point of where you couldn't move, or so fearful to the point of running? This is the fear that Satan wants you to have. A fear that will have you boggled down to where you can't be of any assistant to the kingdom of God. He wants to have you distressed to the point of where your soul, mind and body become sick; sick with physical ailments and with "soulish" bitterness, and to die in it. Gossip's strategy is to cause you to literally lie in a bed of fear and distress. Gossip wants you to believe that you can't make it and you won't make it; with the attitude of "at least not while I'm around." It causes a false view, a view that will make you think that you are crippled, and that something is wrong with you.

"And yet, O Lord, you are our Father. We are the clay, and you are the potter. We are all formed by your hand"—Isaiah 64:8 (NLT).

Let the Devil know that you are not crippled nor are you broken for you have been formed by the hand of the Father. When Gossip tries to weigh on you with distress and fear, combat its spirit with the Word of God.

"For God hath not given us a spirit of fear; but of power, and of love, and of a sound mind" 2 Timothy-1:7 (KJV).

Timothy has prophesied over us with the Word of God! Look at what God has given you. He has given you power to overcome every problem and obstacle that rises itself against you, He has given you love that covers any multitude of sin and He has given you peace that passes all understanding.

Servants of the Almighty, Gossip will use words of intimidation to try to stop you. It will use intimidating looks and body language to try to keep you still. These stairs and giant like movements are trying to make your knees buckle, but I urge you to grab on to the heart of King David! When everyone else was scared of Goliath, he wasn't because he knew who his God was. Align your heart and mind with the word of God, and tell this demon "I have peace! You will not shake me nor break me!" Raise your hands children of God, and praise your God because you're coming out of the grip of Gossip.

Chapter Three

Restraint, an Unwillingness to Move Forward and Confusion

The word Restraint is defined as imprisonment. Gossip wants to imprison you, shackle you down and cause you not to move forward. You may feel like this spirit has you sitting in a "jail" all confused and broken. You may be confused about your anointing, assignment and appointment that has been set by God. Your heart and mind have become muddy and unclear about the purpose and plan that was planted on the inside of you by the Creator of the world. My brother, Gossip's job is to make you feel like you're in a dark place, my sister; it's trying to make you think that there is no way out because its attitude is "ah ha, I got you now!"

Why is Gossip's attitude "ah ha, I got you now?" Because it has been waiting on you to say or do a thing, so it can cause confusion about you to those that are watching you. You better know that Gossip is watching you. It can't figure you out, so it will pick with you to try to get a response out of you. Don't give Gossip a response! Children of God, Gossip wants to make you feel like you're a bundle of confusion and mess when you know you've been walking in the truth. Gossip is a dream killer and a doubter; it tries to under mind that you really are. Remind Gossip of who you are!

"But you are a chosen people, a royal priesthood, a holy nation, a people belonging to God, that you may declare the praises of him who called you out of darkness into his wonderful light"—1 Peter 2:9 (NIV).

Saints too many people are telling us what we are not, and that's why it's important that we know the Word of God for ourselves. People have subtle ways of throwing words, things and ideas onto you that don't fit you or belong to you. Don't allow snakes to impose themselves, and for your sake don't allow them to attach. Stand on what is good, true and holy. Know that Jesus is the way, the truth and the Light, and it's what He says that matters in the end. Aren't you glad that Elohim has the final say so for your life? There is no door that Gossip can close that the Lord has opened, there is no blessing that the Lord has given that Gossip can take and there is no mandate by Jehovah that Gossip can kill.

Isaiah 54:17 says, "No weapon that is formed against thee shall prosper; and every tongue that shall rise against thee in judgment thou shalt condemn. This is the heritage of the servants of the Lord, and their righteousness is of me, saith the Lord" (KJV).

Stand up before your enemies with your shoulders straight and your head held high, and proclaim that your righteousness is of the Lord! Declare to the enemy that he can't and won't win. No weapon that He forms against you shall prosper. The weapon of Gossip has lost its "footing," and will not stand. Every tongue that has risen against you to cause damage to your destiny has already been condemned.

Begin to thank the Lord:

Lord, I thank you that my righteousness is of you! I thank you that no weapon formed against me shall prosper! Father, I thank you that I have been chosen! You are great God . . . you are great!

Right now allow the Lord to pour His oil of anointing on you. Let his light shine up on you, and His power rest on you. God and the Devil can't rest in the same place, so as you yield to the power and love of God, the oppression of the Devil has to flee. Restraint, the unwillingness to move and confusion have to go. Gossip has just left the building!

Chapter Four

Discomfort

We all have had moments of discomfort, whether it was someone sitting too closely by us on a bus, wearing pants that were too tight that every time we would sit down, we would have to unbutton them or we might have done something that was a little embarrassing like calling someone by the wrong name. There will always be minor situations of discomfort that you come across, but nothing too detrimental or that you can't bounce back from. Gossip's goal is to make you feel deathly discomfort. It wants you to feel and know that it has told your business, and now everyone it has told your business to is making a spectacle of you.

Gossip will try to taunt and push you in to discomfort. Plain and simple, Gossip is a bully! Have you ever been bullied? Maybe like in elementary, junior high and high school? Gossip wants to bully you throughout your entire life; it just doesn't stop at high school. People and the Devil will forever be in existence to the end of time or until the Lord comes back, until then, Gossip will forever be in rotation.

Here is a funny story. Well . . . I find it to be funny now, but I didn't find it to be so funny at the time. I went to a church where people "proclaimed" to have "assigned" seats, and I sat in a seat that a couple had been sitting in for years. Of course I didn't know that they had been sitting there for so long, and had claimed the seat as being theirs. I was sitting in the seat, and the couple came in and sat beside me. Five minutes into us all getting settled in our seats, the man whispers to me and says "we've been sitting in that seat (pointing to where I was sitting) for five years." Right at that moment I began to feel discomfort, like I was in their seat. Praise and worship began and the guy begin to praise the Lord, and while doing so he would nearly hit me with his hand, or would get so close to me as to push me out in to the aisle. I realized that he was trying to make me feel discomfort because I had sat in "his" seat.

That's Gossip's ploy, it wants to make you move out of your seat. Gossip will have your mind off focus so that you can't enjoy praising the Lord, or that you can't hear the Word of God when it is being preached. Gossip wants to hit you in the face and push you out the way to assure you not to come back.

Something else that I've noticed about Gossip is that it's competitive. It believes that there is only one person that can soar at a time, and obviously that only one is Gossip. If Gossip sees even a hint of the anointing on your life, it won't like you. Tell Gossip "the sky is the limit, and there's room for us all to soar." Listen to what Peter spoke in the house of Cornelius.

"Then Peter opened his mouth, and said, of the truth I perceive that God is no respecter of persons: but in every nation he that feareth him, and worketh righteousness, is accepted with him"—Acts 10:34-35 (KJV).

Peter knew and understood the Lord. It's one thing to know the Lord, but do you understand him? Don't you just hate being misunderstood? A person may know your name, things about you and may even know your character, but that doesn't mean they understand you. Peter had insight because he said, "I perceive." Are you perceiving and truly having insight on that which God is? Peter said that God is no respecter of persons.

Saints, God is no respecter of persons, and whatever he does in your life He can do in another and vice versa. Here is the catch! You have to fear Him and walk in righteousness. God's blessings aren't predicated on who you are, what you look like and what you do; they're predicated on your obedience and righteousness. When Gossip is looking at you funny or talking about you because God is using you in a mighty way just say, "My God is no respecter of persons, and whosoever has their heart set on the will of God, He will use them too." Don't let Gossip move you out of your seat, stay planted!

Chapter Five

Complication and Difficulty

Obstacles can make things complicated and difficult. Sometimes things can get so complicated and difficult to the point to where you want to give up. Gossip's middle name is Obstacle. When Gossip gets involved it seems like everything that you're trying to do has become hard. The so good relationships you thought you had have become strained. People that were once willing to help you don't want anything to do with you anymore. Anything productive that you are trying to do Gossip has found a way to try to see that it fails. It seems like every avenue you try to take Gossip has set up a dead end sign. The enemy wants to see how hard you will work to press pass him.

Such obstacles can cause frustration and anger, and the kind of frustration and anger I'm talking about is the kind that makes you want to fight. Don't be foolish and fight because the battle can't be won by physical war fare.

"And he said, hearken ye, all Judah, and ye inhabitants of Jerusalem, and thou king Jehoshaphat, Thus saith the Lord unto you, Be not afraid nor dismayed by reasons of this great multitude; for the battle is not yours, but God's"—2 Chronicles 20:15 (KJV).

God has your Gossip situation under control, so there is no need for you to fight. Yeah, I know it seems easier and quicker to take your route, but it's not wise. Gossip would love to see you out of control, so it can say to its co-spectators, "look there, I told you so." Don't give them the pleasure of knowing that Gossip has affected you.

Something that I recently learned was that a lot of times we think that if we yell at or fight the devil to flee, he will flee. No my brothers and sisters, your yelling and fighting is just causing the devil to laugh at you. His laughing at you is making you believe that you have no power. You have power! The power is in your silence. Sit back and pray, and discern your situation. Smile at Gossip when it speaks. Say hello to Gossip when you walk in the room, but nothing more. Ignore Gossip and it will flee. Eventually, those that have stirred up Gossip will look like the fool. People will begin to realize and see that Gossip is a manipulator, a liar and disloyal. Who wants to be connected to something that they can't trust, and we all know that you can't trust Gossip. Gossip's friends have come to the knowledge of "if Gossip will tell your business, then it will definitely tell mine." Gossip will eventually be uncovered, and will be left naked for all to see it for the murderer it truly is.

Let's pray:

Jehovah, God even though I'm displeased with the damage Gossip has caused, I'm thankful for the maturity it has produced in my life. I have become stronger and wiser, and have become a better and more equipped disciple for your use. I pray for Gossip. I pray that it will be delivered into your hands. I don't fight this battle for I know that through you, the battle has already been won. In Jesus' name I pray. Amen.

Children of God your road is becoming smoother now. Complication and difficulty have become bound.

Matthew 16:19 says, "And I will give unto thee the keys of the kingdom of heaven: and whatsoever thou shalt bind on earth shall be bound in heaven: and whatsoever thou shalt loose on earth shall be loosed in heaven" (KJV).

The first book of the Gospel states, **"Whatsoever YOU bind and whatsoever YOU loose."** The power is in your tongue. The same power that the creator of the universe used in order to create the world, He has given to you. Open your mouth and bind up Gossip, let it and its middle name Obstacle know that they have no control over you.

Chapter Six

No Support

We all need support. We need support from family, friends, co-workers etc. When we all have support things seems to go a lot smoother, and our lives seem to be a little brighter. Support is like a team. There is so much that can get done if a team works together. A basketball team may have only a slim chance of winning if they all don't work together. If one player is not doing its job, the team will most likely lose.

Just imagine being out in the middle of the ocean in a boat with no paddles. With no paddles, which are your support, you won't be able to get back to shore. You're just stuck out in a big body of water with nothing to drink, no food and nobody, and probably with hundreds if not thousands of sharks. For me, that would be a very scary situation! Gossip wants you to be stuck out in the middle of the ocean with no support. Gossip knows that if you don't have any help it's going to be very hard for you to succeed. If it could, Gossip wouldn't even leave you a boat to sit in while being in the ocean; it would prefer that you drown. With that being said, Gossip is heartless and only thinks of itself. Who in their right spiritual mind would want to see someone drown, be killed or fail? Well, first of all obviously Gossip doesn't possess the mind of Christ. Gossip is only thinking out of a mind of emotion, and a heart of wrath. It is seeking who it may devour. Don't feel that you are alone because anyone that opposes a threat to Gossip, it wants to strike.

Psalm 57:4 says, "My soul is among lions: and I lie even among them that are set on fire, even the sons of men, whose teeth are spears and arrows, and their tongue a sharp sword" (KJV).

In this passage, Gossip is a metaphor of a lion/s. I believe saints of God that if we ever see a lion not caged, you and I both are going to most likely run! But in the case of Gossip, just stand still. Gossip wants to appear to look scary and ferocious, and for its roar to seem loud, but nothing about it possesses power or strength. Gossip acts the way it does because it is weak and fearful. Gossip has no faith, and is fueled by rejection. You really ought to feel sorry for Gossip. It will do whatever it can to gain what it can, whether it's a job promotion, friendships, a spouse, praise . . . whatever. Gossip will always try to stand in the way of your reward. The text up above also says that Gossip's teeth are like darts and arrows, and its tongue is like a sword. Gossip is absolutely reckless! One would think "wow, does Gossip really know how harmful it is?" The answer to that thought is yes it does. Gossip wants you to lose. It wants to shred you to pieces.

When Gossip recklessly pushes you in to a corner of no support realize that it's your time to flourish. It's your time to flourish spiritually, emotionally, financially and mentally. Gossip is challenging you to grow up. Don't worry about your lack of support; this just gives God an opportunity to show Himself mighty. God wants to bring out the Gideon in you. Once you have gotten to your place of purpose, no one not even yourself will be able to have the glory. When you have arrived from destitute to destiny, your enemies will know that your success was of the Lord. Salute your non-supporters, God is about to do something wonderful in your life.

Part 2

Places Gossip will cause You to Run

Chapter Seven

A Place of Desolation

When you think of a place of desolation, what do you think of? My mind goes to a place like a desert where there is no water, no food and no people; only scorching heat and drought. How in the world does one survive in such a place? Many of you may feel like you're in a desert, and you're wondering how do you or will you survive. There's a song that says, "God will be your oasis in the middle of the desert."

Webster's dictionary says that the word desolation is defined as devastation and ruin. Gossip wants to drive you to a place of devastation and ruin. It wants you to be in utter despair, and for your sweetness to become bitter. The enemy knows that if you become bitter because of Gossip and the damage that it has caused, you will walk away from loving people, the call of God on your life and God himself. Now there Satan goes again, he has been able to deceive another one of God's children to join his camp. Satan is saying to your mind, "look at these church folks, I thought they were Christians but all they do is tear each other down." Or he might say, "wasn't he or she supposed to be your friend, and look at how they turned their back on you." There are many things that the enemy will say to try to keep you from hearing the voice of God. Just know that even when Gossip has driven you to a place of devastation and ruin, God has the power and wisdom to bring you out. This is your time to pray and seek Him; this isn't your time to give up. No matter what is going on in my life, I would rather be on the side of the Lord any day than on the side of the enemy. When a place of desolation is surrounding you speak a Word over your life.

Psalm 121:1-2 says, "I will lift up mine eyes unto the hills, from whence cometh my help. My help cometh from the Lord, which made heaven and earth" (KJV).

Growing up, when I would read this scripture, I would wonder "why in the world am I looking to the hills for help?" This scripture didn't make any sense to me, and it hadn't connected with my spirit man. Now when I read these two verses, I know that when I look to the hills or to the heavens there present is the right hand of God ready to fight my battles. Saints of God, we can't look through our natural eyes but we have to look through our spiritual eyes. Knowing God's Word will give you a clearer view of who He is, the access you have to the kingdom of God and to the power of God. The Word of God will also remind you of your value and purpose.

During your spare time read *2 Kings Chapter 6:8-23*, and see how Elisha was brave enough not to run because of the great host of enemies he saw before him, but he chose to stand still because he saw an even greater host of angels that covered him. Gossip wants you to believe that you have no help, but just open your spirit and look to the hills.

Chapter Eight

A Place of Depression

So many people in the world today are walking around depressed and high strung on depression medication. Now, I'm not at all knocking medication because if you need it please use wisdom and take it. I don't want anyone to read this book, and go throw all their medicines away. God wants us to have both faith and wisdom. But I want you to ask yourself, "Why am I depressed?" Is a mental disease the cause of your depression, or is it because of what someone said to you that hurt your feelings? Is it because of how you look or something you don't have? If a mental disease is the cause of your depression, then I would say for sure you would probably need to stay on your medication until your mental healing comes. If you are dealing with depression because of what someone has said or done to you, or because of how you look or because of something you don't have etc., you need to examine the situation. Your happiness and joy shouldn't be predicated on what someone else has told you or thinks of you. Your happiness and joy shouldn't be predicated on what you look like, nor should your happiness and joy be predicated on what you have or don't have.

Nehemiah 8:10 says, "Then he said unto them, go your way, eat the fat, and drink the sweet, and send portions unto them for whom nothing is prepared: for this is holy unto the Lord: neither be ye sorry; for the joy of the Lord is your strength" (KJV).

Don't you know that God has made every day to be holy? For some reason, we think that Sunday is the only holy day. We think that Sunday is the only day to worship God, Sunday is the only day to love our brothers and sisters in Christ, and that Sunday is the only day for families to sit down and have dinner. If God has made every day to be holy don't you know that you can always tap in to His goodness, and all that he has for you. Nehemiah told the people to eat and drink; and to give to those that don't have. There is no reason for you to sit around and be depressed over things that don't matter because knowing who He is, is what matters the most. Get up every day out of Gossip's sorrow, and enjoy your life! There is somebody that needs what you have to give. Know that the joy of the Lord is your strength! The joy of knowing that all your needs are met according to His riches and glory, the joy of knowing that you are the apple of His eye and the joy of knowing that you are more than a conqueror through Him.

Child of God there is something unique on the inside of you. There is something that God has placed in you that is only designed for you. No one can do it like you can. Never think that your anointing is less than or that someone else's anointing is greater. The word, kind act, gift, dance, song etc. from you, somebody is waiting on to help bring them out of bondage. We have to stop comparing ourselves to one another like the world does. Servants of God, YOU have an action of deliverance.

"For we dare not make ourselves of the numbers, or compare ourselves with some that commend themselves; but they measuring

***themselves by themselves, and comparing themselves among
themselves, are not wise"—2 Corinthians 10:12 (KJV).***

Gossip compares itself with another causing itself to become
self-righteous. The word says that our own righteousness is as filthy
rags. Gossip thinks that it is better than everyone else, and when
it tries to come up against you, it will try to cause you to become
unrighteous. Why do I say that? Because like I said in a previous
chapter, Gossip coming at you will want to make you act like a
fool and fight, but don't do it. Tell Gossip "I choose to stay in the
righteousness of the Lord."

Chapter Nine

A Lack of Trust
and
A Lack of Companionship

Now, if Gossip came by way of someone you trusted or you thought was a good person; someone you thought you could confide in or have a mere conversation with but you found out that you couldn't, and now you have a lack of trust and good feelings towards companionship, then Gossip has driven you to a place of distrust of people and/or "friends." First know that not everyone is out to get you, there are actually people that are for you and not against you. God is about to prune your discernment.

"For thou hast made him most blessed for ever: thou hast made him exceeding glad with thy countenance. For the king trusteth in the Lord, and through the mercy of the most High he shall not be moved. Thine hand shall find out all thine enemies: thy right hand shall find out those that hate thee"—Psalm 21:6-8 (KJV).

Children of God when God has blessed and anointed you, some people won't be able to handle your blessing/s, but put your trust in the Lord. The Lord will show you your enemies and those that hate you. He will never let you walk into a situation blind, and know that when he does show you your enemies believe Him. What do I mean by believe Him? There have been situations in my life where God would try to show me that certain friends and people were not for me, but of course I would say or think, "But they are my friend, they wouldn't do that to me or they are a cool person they wouldn't say that about me." But brothers and sisters, they have said and they will say whatever about you, and they have done and they will do whatever to you.

Gossip will come against you with no remorse and no apologies. When God shows you the persons that are not for you, you better get them out of your space, your business and your life quick, fast and in a hurry. Gossip is causing more damage than what you are aware of. Thank God for the wisdom of James.

James 1:5 says, "if any of you lack wisdom, let him ask of God, that giveth to all men liberally, and up-braideth not; and it shall be given him" (KJV).

Ask God for wisdom, He will give it to you without reproach. The Father wants you to make wise decisions about connecting with people that are trying to come into your life. Gossip wants to harm you and not help you. It will come up to you as a wolf in sheep's clothing only wanting to get close enough to you to see the type of person you are, and to learn of your secrets. Once Gossip finds out anything about you, it will run to the masses with their "information." Don't let Gossip keep you from trusting the people that really love you, and that appreciate the God in you.

Chapter Ten

Remoteness of Human Habitation

Gossip will try to have you not wanting to go to work, social functions, to church or wherever there are people. Don't let Gossip send you to a place of remoteness of human habitation. Gossip doesn't want you around because it knows that it can continue the manipulation, the lies and the telling of your business if you're not present to show your true godly character. It believes it can grow by cultivating its own stories of your person (self). Show up to your job, church and social functions, and walk in your God given glory. Your presence shows that you are still standing; your presence shows that Gossip hasn't killed you and your presence shows that God is on your side.

Pushing your way pass Gossip lets spectators know that you are victorious. Pushing your way pass Gossip tells it that "I have work to do and I'm not going to let you stop me." Saints pushing your way pass Gossip works those muscles in you that you never knew you had, and even those that you knew you had but you allowed to get a little fatty. Gossip is strengthening your muscles of prayer, your muscles of reading and studying the Word, your muscles of fasting and your muscles of hearing and knowing the voice of God. Gossip is even strengthening the muscles of your present and future ministry. I know Gossip has caused some major damage, but look at the good it has done and can do in your life. If you allow, Gossip will help to shape you in to a Godly and productive person, and it won't even know it. Look at Gossip and tell it "thank you."

Maybe there are things in you that need to be cleaned out, and if so let Gossip help you. Put it to use for your benefit. God wants you to see that the benefit of Gossip is that it's cleaning your system of deadly waste. What waste? Examine yourself and see. For me, through Gossip, God had to show me that my waste was the wanting to be loved, liked and accepted by people; the waste of wanting to be a people pleaser. I trusted everyone around me thinking that if I treated them good, then they would do the same to me. I was very naïve and gullible, and had a closed eye to those around me. God had to use Gossip to remove the child like spectacles from my eyes. He used Gossip to show me that I was in sin by putting my trust more so in people, rather than in Him. He used Gossip to let me know that even though others may not love me, like me or accept me that He does. He used Gossip to remind me that it doesn't matter if people agree with me, but what needs to be in agreement is my life with His Word. Gossip's intent is to kill you but if you don't die from it, God will promote you to another level. God wants to elevate you. Will you allow Him? Allow Gossip to make His work in you perfect. The process will be painful, but the fruit of it will be bountiful and sweet.

Galatians 6:9 says, "And let us not be weary in well doing: for in due season we shall reap, if we faint not" (KJV).

Part 3

How to Recover From Gossip

The Recovery

"O Lord, by these things men live, and in all these things is the life of my spirit: so wilt thou recover me, and make me live"
—*Galatians 38:16 (KJV)*

I was asked the question of why did I write this book? I wrote this book because I believe that God's heart and desire is to see people recovered and restored from the damage of Gossip. I believe that if we all are aware of Gossip and understood its deathly intent, we all would be careful not to be its tool. There have been so many people that have suffered by the hand of Gossip, and they have no idea on how to recover. God wants you to recover. It is His will that you recover. This is your time. The things that I discussed in each chapter of this book are ways that Gossip tried to affect me, and places where Gossip tried to cause me to run. I was hurt, angry, bitter and confused. I was about to give up on the assignments that God placed in my heart. I was about to leave one of the places that I love being at the most. For me, that place was church. I didn't understand why he allowed this weapon to attack me. I was about to give up on friendships that really meant me well. I felt completely broken and didn't understand why God allowed Gossip to happen. I began to pour my heart out before the Lord. I started back fasting; I began to read and study my Word more, and I began to seek God about every situation. I became wiser and stronger in Christ, and His voice became clearer to me. I started to realize that God used Gossip to push me into another level in Him. My eyes opened to the fact that He used Gossip to process me, and to promote me.

One Sunday morning, I had awakened with a terrible pain in my body. It had come up on me suddenly with no warning. I went to church any way because I really didn't want to miss the service. While at church, I prayed that God would just automatically heal me then and there, but nothing happened. I wound up having to leave church before it even began. I took a trip to the local emergency room; the doctor ran a test on me, diagnosed my problem and prescribed me with medicine. I thought, "Ok. Now I have this pain under control." While driving home, I realized that I didn't have any money to purchase the prescribed medicine. I called one of my sisters and she gave me a home remedy, so I tried it. The remedy was awful nasty and was burning my throat. I thought to myself "God, you got to do something because I can't keep taking this stuff!" I began to quote the Word of God to Him with the attitude of "now this is your Word Lord, you got to obey!" God still didn't stretch out His hand and heal me. The pain persisted and I began to think I was powerless.

One day I was standing in a classroom monitoring students while they were taking a test, and God spoke to me. He said, "If you write, I will heal you." You may be wondering what God meant by that? Well for me, God meant that as I tell my story to heal others, then He would heal me. As you give, you receive. Saints of God there are some emotional, spiritual and mental damages, as well as physical ailments in your body that if you tell your story of the pain you've either been through or are going through God will heal you. He will heal you in the midst of your telling. For me, my story and healing came through my being obedient to write. How will your story be told? In what way will your healing come? Your play, book, poem, song or dance will not only bring about a healing in your life, but will bring about deliverance in another's life.

As I was writing this very book, God begin to heal my body of the illness that was plaguing me. I never even needed a drug or a home remedy. The healing that took place wasn't just for my physical ailment but was also for my heart, mind and soul. I pray children of God that you have recovered from Gossip. You now have power!

5 Steps of Recovery

1. First, know and understand that God allowed Gossip to come against your life.

"And we know that all things work together for good to them that love God, to them who are the called according to his purpose"—Romans 8:28 (KJV).

There is nothing that is done under the sun that the Lord almighty doesn't know about. God didn't allow Gossip to come in to your life without a purpose. A lot of times we ask for God to birth a great anointing on the inside of us, but we ask without understanding the process or the cost. Open the eyes of your heart, and know and understand that Gossip was present to help you grow. It has just catapulted you in to your massive assignment; an assignment that will make a way for many others.

"And Joseph said unto them, fear not: for am I in the place of God? But as for you ye thought evil against me; but God meant it unto good, to bring it to pass, as it is this day, to save much people alive"—Genesis 50:19-20 (KJV).

Gossip's intent was of evil against you, and it thought that once it was done with you that you would never rise again. Gossip thought that since it had thrown you in a pit, you would never get out. O' but how I praise God for His resurrecting power! God allowed you to go through the fire because He knew that you wouldn't break. He knew that someday you would be able to testify before man, and that your testimony would bring life to their broken and dead places. Joseph knew that the wicked deed of his brothers toward him was just a set up for him to be in place during a season of famine. Saints, God has just used Gossip to set you **in place** for a season of famine. He has called you to be His hands, His feet and His mouth in a dry and weary land. People are thirsty for love and truth, and by his power and Word; you have been called to quench the thirst.

2. Pray, fast, read and study God's Word more.

"And Moses called all Israel, and said unto them, Hear, O Israel, the statues and judgments which I speak in your ears this day, that ye may learn them, and keep, and do them"
—Deuteronomy 5:1 (KJV).

Hearing, reading and studying God's word on a constant basis helps us to know the desires of the Lord, as well as helps us to hear His voice clearer. Once we know the voice of the Lord, we have no excuse not to follow and trust Him.

"My sheep hear my voice, and I know them, and they follow me"—John 10:27 (KJV).

3. Go back to the place where Gossip had driven you from.

"Thou preparest a table before me in the presence of mine enemies; thou anointest my head with oil; my cup runneth over
—Psalm 23:5 (KJV).

Go back to work, to church, to social events and to the family reunion. Once Gossip sees you it will realize that your life is orchestrated by the hand of God, and that's why you're still alive and well. It will realize that it hasn't killed you. Saints the devil can't kill that which is of God, from God and is God's. I encourage you to go back! God has prepared a place for you in the presence of your enemies.

4. Stand in silence.

"The Lord shall fight for you, and ye shall hold your peace"
—Exodus 14:14 (KJV).

I know that you have your way of wanting to fight Gossip, but seek the Lord instead. God's way and wisdom will always prevail. Silence shows Gossip your true strength so stand or better yet, sit back and relax; let the Lord fight your battles.

5. Finally, continue to do the work of the Lord.

"That he would grant unto us, that we being delivered out of the hand of our enemies might serve him without fear, in holiness and righteousness before him, all the days of our life"
—Luke 1:74 (KJV).

You have been delivered from the fear of Gossip! Serve the Lord, your God in holiness and righteousness; serve Him in joy. You have surpassed your enemies; now walk in to your destiny.

Let's pray:

Lord, I thank you for my recovery. You have restored my soul, and have caused me to stand again. God, I stand in your perfect peace. I thank you that Gossip hasn't killed me, but has only drawn me closer to you and has set me on my assigned seat of destiny. God I return from the place I had run to, and I run back into your arms. In Jesus' name, I pray. Amen.

Contact Information:

Phone: (318)-581-2997

Email: jacquelinestewart1447@yahoo.com